Michael Phelps

by Grace Hansen

Abdo
OLYMPIC BIOGRAPHIES
Kids

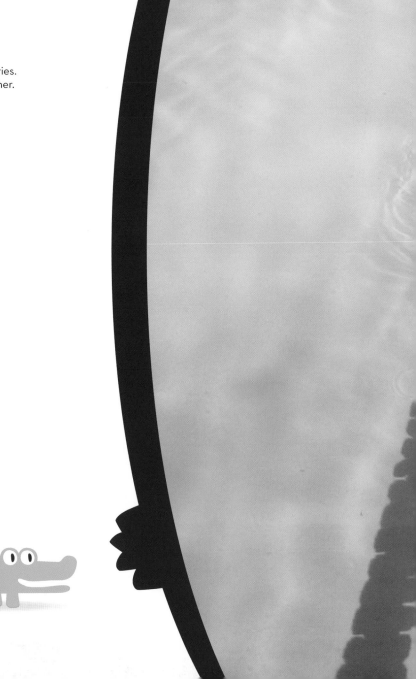

abdopublishing.com

Published by Abdo Kids, a division of ABDO, PO Box 398166, Minneapolis, Minnesota 55439.

Printed in the United States of America, North Mankato, Minnesota.

102016

012017

 THIS BOOK CONTAINS RECYCLED MATERIALS

Photo Credits: Alamy, AP Images, Getty Images, iStock, Shutterstock

Production Contributors: Teddy Borth, Jennie Forsberg, Grace Hansen

Design Contributors: Laura Mitchell, Dorothy Toth

Publisher's Cataloging-in-Publication Data

Names: Hansen, Grace, author.

Title: Michael Phelps / by Grace Hansen.

Description: Minneapolis, MN : Abdo Kids, 2017. | Series: Olympic
    biographies | Includes bibliographical references and index.

Identifiers: LCCN 2016952608 | ISBN 9781680809459 (lib. bdg.) |
    ISBN 9781680809503 (ebook) | 9781680809558 (Read-to-me ebook)

Subjects: LCSH: Phelps, Michael, 1985- --Juvenile literature. | Swimmers--
    United States--Biography--Juvenile literature. | Olympic athletes--
    United States--Biography--Juvenile literature. | Olympic Games (31st : 2016 :
    Rio de Janeiro, Brazil)--Juvenile literature.

Classification: DDC 797.2/1092 [B]--dc23

LC record available at http://lccn.loc.gov/2016952608

Table of Contents

Early Years

Michael Phelps was born on June 30, 1985. He grew up near Baltimore, Maryland.

4

Baltimore

Phelps started swimming at a young age. He competed in his first Olympics at age 15. He did not win a medal. But it was the start of a **legendary** career.

6

It didn't take long for Phelps to start winning races. He broke the 200-meter fly record in 2001.

Athens!

Phelps competed in the 2004 Olympic games. He swam the 400-meter **IM** in record time. He left Athens, Greece, with eight medals.

11

Beijing!

The 2008 Olympics were even better for Phelps. He won eight gold medals. No other athlete had done that at one Olympics.

London!

Phelps took home six medals from the 2012 Olympics. He now had 22 Olympic medals. That was a record!

Rio and Retirement

Rio 2016 would be Phelps's last Olympics. He was ready to **retire**. He wanted to make a splash!

16

Phelps did just that. He won

six medals. Five were gold!

18

Phelps competed in five Olympic games. He has 28 Olympic medals. His gold medal count is 23. Until someone can beat that, Phelps is the greatest Olympian.

21

More Facts

- Michael Phelps is built to swim. He is 6 feet, 4 inches (2m 10cm) tall. His torso is long and thin. His legs are short in comparison to his size 14 feet, which act like flippers.

- Phelps's wingspan is longer than he is tall. Tip to tip measures 6 feet, 8 inches (2m 20cm).

- At 15, Phelps was the youngest swimmer to compete in the Olympics in nearly 70 years.

Glossary

IM – short for individual medley, which is a race involving four different swimming styles: the breaststroke, backstroke, butterfly stroke, and freestyle.

legendary – very famous and well-known.

retire – to stop a career because you do not need or want to do it anymore.

Index

abdokids.com

Use this code to log on to abdokids.com and access crafts, games, videos, and more!

Abdo Kids Code:
OMK9459

24